ZAHRA ABDUL RAZAQ

Secrets of Teens

First edition

ISBN: 9798581432594

Cover art by Anna Pham

This book was professionally typeset on Reedsy.
Find out more at reedsy.com

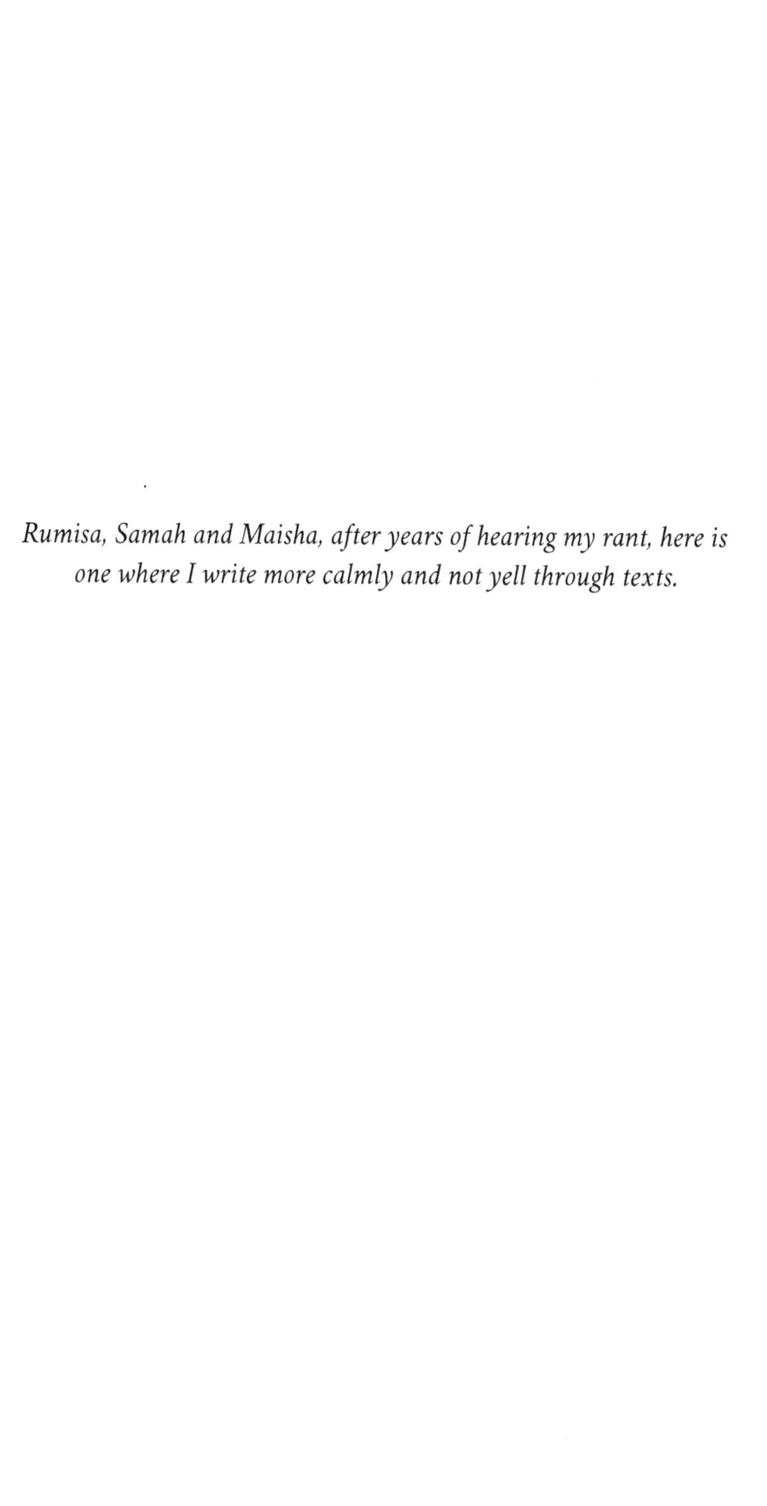

Rumisa, Samah and Maisha, after years of hearing my rant, here is one where I write more calmly and not yell through texts.

There is only way to happiness and
that is to cease worrying about things
which are beyond our power.

EPICTETUS

Contents

Acknowledgement

Completing a book had taken a lot of time and effort, and there were many people behind the screen who had helped this to come to life.

I would like to thank my parents for supporting me from writing the drafts all the way to publishing it. Thank you for giving me the tools I needed to transform it into what it is today. There are no words to thank you for giving me all the support I needed.

I would also like to thank Imran and Irfan, my two elder brothers whose characters in this book have been joined into one. They have let out cheesy jokes and some failed attempts while trying to initiate me when I am writing on my writing desk.

My younger sister, Sarah, who has helped me with my errands and made my life a little more comfortable by getting me a glass of water when I am too lazy to move an inch. She has made me write freely, without any worries.

My classmate, Maleeha for reading my short writing and giving me suggestions that help me turn into a better writer. Being of the first to always read it, her constructive criticism is what I have been longing to receive, and she was there to make my wish come true.

A big thank you to Anna Pham helping me with the cover. She had helped me with the cover several times and there is nothing I could say to show my gratitude.

Finally, to all school teachers, helping me find my voice. To, Ms Janette Lawrence and Ms Rashmi Harish who have cleared my doubts numerous times and has been patient with all my inquiries. Two of the pillars which made this dream of mine come true, truly there are no words to describe their support.

Ms Janet Pinheiro and Ms Sujitha Manoharan, whose confidence and passion for teaching is clear as crystal helped me find my love for a type of art I didn't know I appreciated. I have been blessed to be having so many great teachers into making me a better person.

Prologue

There I was. I was babbling to my mother about how annoying my older brother, Aaron, is. Mother shakes her head and said, "I'll tell him to stop".I happily left the kitchen realising that Mother would reprimand Aaron that day for disturbing me once more. Aaron had always done something that made me clench my teeth in anger. Whether it would be leaving the door open, talk loudly while I am speaking to my friends or when he changed the channel I am watching for some action-filled movie, he knows how to get the worse of me.

Let's start by introducing ourselves? My name is Ashley. A word that means genuine in English was the name my cousins liked more. They wanted the name Ashley more. Another character had to be in the documents of mine before changing it last minute. Hua.

My cousins wanted to name me after a noticeable artist who had gotten numerous honours for her tunes. My mom had then conversed with my aunt the following day to recommend another name before presenting the official papers. My aunt, at that point, concurred with her point. Here comes the energising occasion!

In Odorn and our home, we have the tradition of chucking large amounts of chocolate. When divulged and the name is confirmed, we celebrate it. Age ranging from young kids all the way to adults all come to the compact, exuberant event. Elders of the house usually start the minor events, give a list of names, and ask those around them if they had regarded the name. My aunt's name is also Ashley in her documents.

I had paid a visit to a country that goes by the name of Odorn. We had reasoned that this was the sheltered the country had ever been. Every time at the airport, there was always an itch. From our phone being deprived of their batteries to our impediment getting lost, we could not arrive there with no problem.

We would get out of the airport immediately as we never predict what would happen. My dad's hand signs would call a taxi driver, and he would pick us. Since I was a toddler, I used to sit on my mother's lap due to the lack of space. My cousins and their moms used to come with us. There wasn't a single second where my head wouldn't bump at the ceiling of the car. I then turned behind to see my younger cousins encountering the same thing, and we all cracked into a fit of giggles.

We reached our home and waved goodbye to my cousins as I had known I wouldn't meet them until our summer holidays of kindergarten would be over. We knocked on the green-coloured door before seeing Barry, an older cousin of mine who was always on my last nerves, opened the door and exclaimed loudly to everyone that we had arrived.

My grandmother engulfed me in hugs and kisses. I shyly used to sit beside my grandmother as she would talk with my mother. I would forget the name of my cousins (my mom's nieces and nephews), and they would shake their head if I had gotten it wrong and would nod if I got it right. I once remember going upstairs to call Ava for dinner.

"Ava, mom said you need to come downstairs to have dinner" I looked at her as she kept her school project in her drawer, which later on she told me she worked on for a month!

She shook her head and grinned. I kept on calling her repeatedly before thinking she could not hear me. I left a gigantic sigh after not getting a response from her, and she left out a small giggle.

"Wait a minute! You are Ravin, right?" she started laughing once she realised I recognised her. My cheeks were glowing red. I had never felt more embarrassed.

They would never let me come close to the door. If it was the ice cream man with his cart hitting the bell or if it was the neighbours, they would not allow me no matter what. Whenever the girls would come from school, we would keep a bucket of water near, and once the door handle giggled, we threw a bucket of water right into their faces.

Ravin and the other girls would chuckle while trying to dry their hands off on their uniforms, making their black-and-white uniform (in which almost all schools wore the same colours) would get wet. Throwing water was fun and exciting until mom told us to stop since they would fall ill. I am amazed to see that they didn't throw a fit over it. If it had been me, I would not have appreciated it at all, whether it was a 3-year-old or a young adult.

They would buy me ice creams too often. Whether it was day, night, or evening, I would have ice cream. The chocolate and fruit-flavoured were my favourites; however, those were also the ones who melt quickly under the scorching sun, and I would paint my face with artificial colour. There was almost an ongoing joke in our family that I feed my entire face while having an ice cream.

If mom did not allow ice cream, what other snacks would we have? Chips! There were these puffy cheese sticks that were about a finger tall, and in each packet, there would either be a hair clip, sticker, a small image colouring thing, or nuts. I would pay for the gifts mainly, and the chips' tasted like dipping a stick in a bowl full of cheese.

They would pay for many snacks and food. Once my uncle bought a considerable amount of apricots for everyone. I had an enormous number of them. The flavour was just not enough. There is no harm in a young girl loving fruits. What is the worst that could happen?

I had gotten queasy, and so did Kassie to the point we came

back home. Since I was not feeling well, all I wanted was to go back and sleep. I remember my grandma dropping us at the airport. I had thought I would just come back the next year. What I didn't know was that that might have been the last time until I had been a teenager again.

I remember going back home, entering my room, before taking two steps back. Before running the fastest, I had ever jumped. I had gotten a new bed. A bigger one this time. With the classic cover of gold and white, I had jumped and jumped, ruining the bed covers. I was thanking my dad while repeatedly jumping on the bed. That was one of the best nights of my life.

Together, those few months are just extraordinary. The condition now makes me sad, knowing that I might never have the chance to get to know my country, sit under the shades, or walk freely in the green parks or high up the snowy mountains. Just one day, that dream of mine might come true.

Back here in Amstone, my life wasn't that boring. With two adoring parents by my side and one elder brother, including a younger sister, we excelled in our academics. Maybe not so much from Aaron and Kassie, but we were thriving.

Aaron and Kassie were my two other siblings. They were excellent in extracurricular activities, or as our family likes to call it, activities that are not included in the overall report card activities.

Dad used to take us weekly to this kid's arcade place known as 'Fun Lake,' and I would lie if I say that was not the highlight of my childhood. Every Friday, I would wait for my dad to tell me to inform all kids to get ready at ten to go to heaven for us.

I remember joyfully exclaiming about it to my cousins, two of our older cousins also joining us in going to the arcade mostly for them to be with us so we could guide them while they had fun.

Those weekends always ended with my dad buying us some ice cream, usually the Classic vanilla, or some fries that would get dipped in ketchup. Sometimes he would buy us these chicken sandwiches with apple and mango juice, which was much needed under the scorching sun of Amstone.

Chapter One

Now I don't exactly recollect all of my childhood. All I remember is my dad taking us to festivals with those long rides, and you slide it. The inflatable ones were filled with air. Those are a few memories I would never forget.

My dad recorded it in his newest edition 2000s sliding phone, in which in one video you can see me bawling my eyes out and angrily spitting harsh words about the much older guy who pushed me from behind and made me fold my legs and slide while also shoving the kid in front of me and hitting my head because I was busy crying and babbling to my dad.

The kid before me also started sobbing because of how badly I kicked her from behind. The force of being nudged from a 2 feet high slide is rough. I felt bad for the other girl, but instantly after that happened, all I remember doing is just yelling at the guy while dad was hugging me and comforting me.

You can hear my dad in the clip going, "What's wrong? What happened?" but I was too busy speaking in another language, so the guy ran away. I guess I was frightened to even when I was five.

And at around this time, another younger special version of me was born, Kassie. Now Kassie is athletic, which I was for the first four years of my school. She has nice features and also something which I can never have—the talent for drawing.

Now I'm serious. Some people say, "Oh, I can't draw! I just join lines, and something happens," and next you know, there is a portrait of Emma Watson. Now, they might say that for being humble, sure. That's no problem. Self-discipline is important for a person, too.

Some gasconade on us, these are the terrible people right there. You can show off your art, but graciously do not injure my emotions. Letting out things like, "Is that even a drawing?", I mean thank you for announcing the same feeling that went through my mind when I first picked up a pencil.

And then there is me. Who thinks I can draw something exceptional only to see a broken tooth, ripped out a dress, and my grandma's curtains. When I say I can't draw, I mean I really can't only if I put the work and effort into it, which the vitality of it only comes five times a year.

Not going to be lying; I made some creative art here and now back when I was younger. Now it seems like astronomical talent has run away to another place. The fact that I can't draw isn't even the biggest problem. Sure, there are over seven billion humans on earth; not all can draw Paris Hilton.

Almost everyone in my family can draw, which makes me more embarrassed about my artistic skills. From the eldest member of our family to the younger ones, everyone can.

So basically, every human being I am connected to can all draw. But then the thing is, I care about sometimes drawing when all of my cousins gather around. Only and only then. When all of us come together, and we would have to draw something, I would reach into my pocket and take out the glass item and play behind a small screen.

Getting to grow my empire or a high school is more entertaining than drawing because I can't draw. If I could draw, I would probably not even write. I would be on my table all day.

They are chatting about textures and colour while thinking about which couch to use for my home inside the small screen. Perhaps I don't have the drawing DNA in my blood. I have something else that not everyone else in my family enjoys, that is composing short stories on events that will never occur.

I finished fourth at a school competition back in middle school. I know what the sentence was and what we had to complete after it. "In the dark hallway, I saw a shadow with loud whisperings," or an opening line similar to that line. I inscribed how the principal himself was halting the school regulations and how he is deceiving behind the school's backs. Only for the major character, Hailey went forward to see his dad, who was helping at school, was remedying the light bulb.

Looking back on it now, my story had no significance at all. It was just something written in half an hour by an 11-year-old who had no curiosity in any other activities. Some of all 13 contestants competing with me in my team somehow appointed me because, seemingly, I got the elevated score. 18/20.

I remember just being ecstatic on the way to the lesson before my teacher imploring me if I was going for the last round or not. I jumped excitedly, claiming that they had picked me and I was going for the last round. Everyone cheered, and I thanked them.

Thankfully, my classmates didn't glance at my story, or I didn't know how to confront them.

The trip from school to home wasn't all happy because I felt disappointed that I couldn't be in the top three. It was my first time in a competition, and I was so excited to win a prize or a position only to get fourth place. The entire car ride made me zoned out a bit.

My dad then noticed this and said that I had applied a bigger deal than winning a position.

"First, fourth place is not bad at all. Even if you could not get in the last round, we would be proud of you. You were so nervous about applying and looking at you, ending it with a fourth position and getting rid of your fear," dad patted my back and told me not to worry, to come and have lunch.

That day, the words of my dad struck me. I might not have won it, and I might not even be creative, but then I got rid of my fear. It's not every day you go out and say, "I am not scared anymore."

That's when I realized it's not about winning, but it's about getting over your fear and telling the organizers that you wanted to take part. It is astonishing to have won in front of the pack, yet I didn't. I learned not to rebuff myself for not winning a simple honour.

I didn't push over the edge and questioned my story. I just closed that small section of my life happily, and I would not change for anything. That was a learning experience for me.

I learned I will not always get what I want, and I may not even get a fourth place next time, and it's okay. I will keep working more and more because, as they say, the entire world tries to help you get it if you want something.

Chapter Two

And there I was. In school, I was mentally asking students around me to be calm when they reached the class. Three people came into the class. Let's categorize them into three groups.

One, there were the students who just quietly come in without uttering a word, until you starting a conversation. I was this student until 7:30 where my friends would come in one by one, and I would catch up with them from homework to the school's announcements.

These are the sensible understudies since it is so quiet in the homeroom, especially when I feel worn out from yesterday's homework. I liked these students since it was peaceful with only them around as they come to read their storybooks, complete notes, or just lay their heads and sleep.

Two, the students who yell and high-five everyone on every

step they take. I know some of you all will resemble, 'I was this understudy!' And if you think like that, I am sorry, but I thoroughly disliked those. They are just too loud, and sometimes I can be them, so I guess I don't like myself at times.

Morning is to relax your brain, not to listen to things like,

"So, did you watch the last episode?"

"Ay, I watched it on the spot, okay?"

I really couldn't care less about your morning coffee, your love for Christina's friendships, or where you went on the weekend.

I may sound discourteous, and I am grieved. I truly possibly care about that when I am in my outgoing individual mode and completely have nobody to converse with for topics that interest both of us. At that point, I need your loud voices, individuals.

Then, the people who drop their friends off at their classes so they wouldn't get lost. Like seriously, I vow you, your friend won't get lost by a mere Sunday morning after being here for years. I'm truly grieved. I didn't intend to pour out your mysteries that way. Or maybe I am writing this as I feel true envy since none of my classmates did it for me.

Now the classrooms reminded me of one of the biggest environmental problems. How do we explain this side of the already polluted world? The classrooms are good if you ask me; white walls, golden brown doors, a long locker for the *teacher*, benches, and tables.

Now notice how I used the word "lockers for teachers" tilted? That's because, in almost all cartoons, movies, series, you name it, there are lockers for the student. It is for the students to place their books, and it's for them to decorate.

But where? The lockers are for the teachers to put the quiz papers, shiny decorative papers for the outside board. Extra pens and pencils also found their way there. Honestly, in the teacher's staff room, there are lockers for them too.

It's not something I would keep if I were the principal. I would want to make lockers for students. Allow loud volumes of sunlight to present. And most definitely to fix the AC. It would only work for the students sitting in the back, and those in front would fan themselves with their textbooks.

So, they get two lockers while we students get one. One as in the one has at home, which is most likely rationed by your siblings. I hope schools assess this and make some lockers for their students because having eight subjects with textbooks and notebooks can get heavy on some days of the week.

But on the other side, we shouldn't discredit them. 'Teacher's pet' was the name given to my new classmate, Vanessa, in school by my friends. At first, I gave no attention to it, but as time passed, vexation and pique filled their eyes, and I felt those teasing eyes were lost.

That's when I realized when things had gotten a little wrong. Many misunderstandings were all scattered in front of us. At some point, I had developed this feeling of anger. I had thought they were mad at me for Vanessa's actions since I had been her peer at the time.

And honestly, I couldn't be more mistaken.

They had looked after her while I had impeached them for mistreating her feelings purposely. They had thought of Vanessa while I had thought of my perceptions. They were there for the new student, and I wasn't. I felt like I lied to myself after seeing them talk about what had gone wrong.

I understand now I made a mistake. I had learned a valuable lesson, and this and the outcome was worth it. I had blindly asked my friends to take care of the way they speak, while in reality, they were trying to make things better for Vanessa.

I admit it. I made many mistakes during high school, from my low grades in Science and Maths to crying myself to sleep. I had done it all. In anger, it seems almost too easy to spit any harsh words without feeling remorse.

Though one does not mean what they mean, the words they say will impact their feelings and mind. I was once told to apologize to a student because I was told that I was wrongly teasing students.

Once, just after Middle School started, I was being accused of bullying made me so furious. I remember biting my tongue to control the statements they were throwing at me. Once the class got over. I remember coming on the way back, confronting them that lying was not okay.

I was asked to clarify whether I had hurt a student's feelings accidentally. To this day, I haven't spoken to her. I did. We both knew what we were doing, and nothing else came out of our mouths. In anger, I said that if we both remain friends, there is only one thing we both will get. And that is ultimately hurting both of us.

I think we both had made a decent decision of breaking contacts. I had lost a friend in the middle of big chaos, but I would rather have myself in pain now than later afterwards.

I had battled with a few of my siblings, or I might have done it with each of them. I knew every Saturday as "Fight Day" as that's the day Aaron made the most mistakes, and mom would correct. Or Aaron and I used to argue. There was also something that my mom had to come in from the kitchen to put us in different rooms.

I wasn't a fortunate student. Not until the last year of middle school. I dreaded coming to school. I wanted to get my education in that paper to clarify that I have graduated from my education.

During the second year of Middle School. I came across the word 'mental health.' The word that is driving my force for learning Psychology. I got interested. I search online to see the quantity of money spent on the residents' mental health in Odorn. Only to come across a PDF that showed that no money is being spent on it.

That is the day I wanted to finish my education and study

further Psychology. I soon discussed with my mother my ambitions. She had given me the most devastating information ever that the residents deemed therapy a place for mentally ill individuals.

That sorrow was a word that moved towards the industry and was something only characterized in movies. My mother doesn't believe in this. It is said that citizens from Odorn acknowledged this. It is tragic to see some of my classmates identify themselves as pessimistic.

I am very adequately familiar with what they might be, and not everyone shows the same indications. I know there are some people whose own family members tell them to stop the act. And that is valid.

Those who say it to get a mere reaction from their peers is unfair in my eyes. These individuals wrap the fact that those who need help are just paying scrutiny to the trend. It's sad to see that these things have practically become quite a 'trend.' I truly wish for all to become satisfactory and feel competent because you are. Everyone is stunning from the inside out.

It's okay to have days where you are unhappy. Normalization of vulnerability should be present. It almost seems like these feelings and conditions are only for the unstable. The number is being constantly increased for the number of individuals gone away. The school seems to throw every blame on social media.

The school plays a major role in the mindset of students. There might be teachers who are loving and fun. Few prioritize proper education instead of just merely passing.

The first position is what everyone we knew focused on to get the victorious title. "Let's see who completes this equation first." It's more about speed than learning the concepts. It fixes every question for a time limit. 'Delayed' was the term used for those who could not complete it by the time given.

It seems like the Music Industry is enclosing the mental backing adults should give their precious ones. Some artists speak with their audience with just an instrument. Some artists speak with their fans in another language. Yet, the love and support between them are so powerful that they clarify their songs.

I adore the piano and even though I cannot play it, listening to the piano version of songs is fascinating yet steady. I have always wanted to understand the piano. Though that dream of mine has been futile, my friends have been able to do it. Evelyn was one of them.

She used to bring her keyboard during music classes and used to practice behind every student. Those beautiful notes are getting encircled by the loud talking of students.

Another glorious memory of school was the trips. These were kind of like a necessity to do. First, enter the bus with enormous smiles and your bag or backpack replenished with snacks and drinks. Drinks that are presumably water and juices, no cold drinks.

Snacks were usually the main three. What were the main three?

Chips, chocolates or candies and some drinks with it. Or maybe our groups of friends used to do this. We would already pre-plan our partners and groups before going to the event.

The back students at the bus would sing songs everyone usually attended on the bus. There would be laughs, jokes, and games during the forty-five-minute bus ride. The bus time was the most underrated time of the entire trip.

The trips were always fun. There is no doubt about that. Half of our time, we would spend by us running around the place. Every year we would make recent memories in every new location we would go.

Then the bus back to school. There were two categories of students. Those were tired and used to doze off until the bus reached a bumpy corner of the road or the irritable ones who thought the trip expired too quickly. I was obviously in the second category of students only because those four hours were over in a blink of an eye.

School trips were just a fresh experience.

Chapter Three

In class, there are three rows of seats or usually, that is the number of rows in the rooms we have been assigned to. The first horizontal lines were of students who either love to put their head down in books or is a study buddy.

The next rows are funny students. My friends are the ones that usually sit here and during a break, all we do is laugh and our lunches are half-eaten.

The last rows of students are those who are either very good at studies or is a quiet student. It's nice to be in the back because the air conditioner is working. If only, you have a good pair of eyes, its the best seat in the entire class.

However, if you have weak eyesight and don't have glasses, its the most uncomfortable seat ever. I usually sat in back, not because I was smart or quiet but because I was tall and would be in the presence of other students behind me.

I would sit in front of the class, only to be able to see clearly before being asked to sit in the corner near the white cold walls.

I didn't want to sit in front either. If the teachers wanted ti to showcase an example of neat notebooks, they would ask those in front and I would have to show them my incomplete notebook. Or, when they crack a joke and you have no way around but to giggle to not seem disrespectful.

During lunchtime, we would be having our food in the classroom. If you are in class, you probably wouldn't smell anything and would think it smells like usual.

But if you go out for a moment or when the next teacher came, it used to smell sweet because of the Nutella, spicy because of curry and naan, sour because of all the other smells coming together.

The teacher would put the garbage can in the middle of the door so that the smell would get out. Decrease the temperature, open the window and hold their nose. The students in the back used to suffer because of the cold air. Meanwhile, those in front used to fan themselves since it would work only in one corner.

Not always would we have time to complete our lunch? Sometimes, we would spend those fifteen minutes completing the notes of the next class which was the deadline.

The school boards were one of the most exciting activities for the first month of our school. Every student used to pour out their ideas. We would get all kinds of paper, glue and colour.

Everyone would be busy, either cutting, glueing or attaching something. It's always fun. The teacher would assign every student to do any work, no one would be allowed to sit around.

During the break time, there would be few students out in the corridors, walking while eating their food. Some sit in the back and read a book, while we would come together to eat together and share funny stories.

Macey, a friend of mine since elementary school. We first met during a writing competition. She had gotten runner up position while I had gotten the third position. Ever since that day, we had become great friends.

Macey and I would spend the entire time laughing at some dumb things we had done. We weren't the nicest people when we first met.

She was quite competitive. Overly confident in her work of writing that always made me want to get a higher position than her. But her writing was of no match to mine. She would always write a lovely poem after classes every day.

" The one high up

Looking out the window

Wishing to lay foot on the soft grass

Light wind inviting her to reach out

Holding her hand out

Only to put it back

Once remembered her position as a leader

In the other realm

Laid down in the cold streets

As the rain pours

Along with the drips from eyes

Hands grasping the thin blanket

Soft murmurs of prayer

Leaves the chapped lips of the undeserving "

Macey always loved naming her poems by single words. This poem of hers was named "despondency". She likes to write a page and a half poems.

Macey and I share similar hobbies. Such as asking numerous questions during classes. Especially in the English class. Only because English teachers give a two-word question, a paragraph worth of answer.

They always connect some time of their lives with the answers they give. This could either be in the benefit of students or those who have little time could be in for a lifetime's session.

But it's amusing to see them answer contently at times. I appreciate their effort to trying to make it as clear as possible yet at times, it's quite hard.

When answering a question, there is just one time in a blue moon they say, "You're right". Most of the time, their replies to your answer would be, "You're on the right track" or "It's not incorrect, elaborate more".

Well, now I know why I usually scoreless during English exams. While distributing the papers, our instructors often encourage us to ask them regarding the marks or if they missed a point.

And among only subjects, English is the subject I usually was in line with. I would ask why I had lost a point in a question and they would answer that my answer wasn't clear. And had I written an in-depth answer, I would have gotten all marks easily.

The next time I had done this, given by the advice of my teacher. During the check-up, I was once again met with the loss of my points. I once again encountered her and asked her as to why I once again lost marks.

This time I had gotten the opposite answer I got the last time. "Ashley, my dear. For a 2 point question, you have written half a page answer. After all, a student should know how much to write"

She patted me in the back and left to go to the teacher's lounge while I stood there blankly with my paper in my hand. I am either told that my answers are too short or too long.

I decided to give up and write to my heart's content. If I felt the answer was enough, I would conclude it right there. But, if I felt the answer needed a little more than a few lines, I would write it down.

Surprisingly enough, out of all the three tests that were taken this was the one I had gotten an excellent score and was actually praised by my teacher.

I had learnt something that took me almost a year. To take matters in your hand is not an issue.

Chapter Four

In my life, I had plunged so deep into this hole. I was not myself. My purpose was that year, last year of Middle School was to be this perfect student, had notes ready, was on top of her game, and more. I managed that for three months before the summer holidays.

I just had to be some other girl that I knew I could not be. That other girl that I was imitating broke me, in such a way that I tired of doing nothing. Even when I was doing something, it drained me.

Those three months were exhausting, but I reaped the trust of two people. The people around seemed delighted with me. They all were happy with the new change of attitude that I had and this new personality thing I was going for: top grades, good manners, and a little quieter me. I could take on jokes without coming back at them.

Yet, I felt different. It felt like I was in the body of someone else. Summer holidays made a light bulb glow; I am not myself.

Summer holidays, it was rolled by very quickly. Eight weeks of complete wastage, destruction, and am trying to do soul searching. I had the gadget I loved most of my hand, a phone. It had loads of games on it. I played many games from killing a zombie to growing my empire, all of that.

I had danced to all kinds of songs, from hip-hop to traditional themes. Maybe not as good as a professional dancer, but enough for me to shake myself and relish the moment.

Then, inside my backpack were rolls of homework. Messy pens and dirty erasers were sitting below my books. Some way or the other, I pulled it off and completed it all. The enormous task of the summer holidays: homework? Check. There is a saying between teenagers, 'The internet is everyone's best friend.'

That's why there were rolls of paper because I hadn't reached my bag in weeks! It had been eight months, yet an inch moved nothing.

Now, this is when I woke up in a place I had never known I could exist in. The internal problems of a family can tear down a child, a thirteen-year-old in such away. With the constant fights, tears, arguments, I could not catch up anymore. It's family, right? All siblings argue with each other. There was another realm of the world that I was hiding away from.

The social media. That year, my friends kind of grew apart for a reason I did not understand. There were days that I was too tired to communicate, believing that I am right, and others are wrong. These thoughts of mine put significant friction into our relationships.

Coming from a family that has terrible anger and cannot accept no as an answer, this was the outcome. I did not want to hurt my friends more by irresponsible actions, so all I did was push everyone away and put my head down to study.

I had to put myself in a corner and pull myself together. We were thinking a little while more. It was all my errors that had caused all the disputes. And I was wrong. I thought of myself all along, not thinking about others how others had seen me from a different perspective. That not everyone agreed on is the right one. It changed my thinking.

Day after day, I had to hear comments like, "You have changed so much,". "You were so much better when the year started," "You gained a lot of weight a sudden," "Stop acting like a brat," and so, so much more.

No matter how I behaved, and what I was saying, everyone told me I was incorrect. I just could not discern how everything was perfect, and it all got ruined in such a paltry amount of time. I was being overlooked despite the activities I was doing.

Everyone was despicable and was all over the place until two weeks into school. Until then, all you could hear was the uncertainty in the rooms, glares, quiet rooms unexpectedly being noisy with everyone fighting over their rights.

What my relatives were yelling was the truth. There is just no one to soothe them down and to tell them they were right and that they will get what they had wanted for years. But just nobody knew that about fate. And this is precisely why I just don't like to think about the future.

You work on this dinner full of dishes for your mom to come home and see. You have made a delicious spaghetti with tomato sauce beside it. A glass full of her favourite juice and you have made some brownies or cake.

What is the next step? Of course, you are pacing to walk around the house, waiting to hear the sound of the keys, and directly run to welcome your mother. Your mother, who had a long day, still hugs you back and gives you a soft smile.

She caresses your head before sighing, missing the aroma of her child and her home. You lead the way to show her to the kitchen to show her the dishes you have made her. She gives you a small smile and thanks to you before going to change her clothes to eat the food you have made.

You are pleased that she came home, healthy, and happy. But you can't hide the slight bump in your heart. You had thought she would go and would smile big while engulfing in a hug quickly and immediately tasting some of that delicious brownie you have made.

But that didn't happen, did it? You can make the gifts you want and stun your loved ones. Avoid comprehending their reactions to a particular activity because that might not just go your way.

One way of exhibiting your emotions into activity is writing. You could either express feelings or a novel that would either make some cry before they go to sleep or laugh at 3 am. Or you could build someone's confidence with a self-help book. The likelihoods are just endless.

And honestly, I had my short space. I am not confident others did, though. I had a little tiny world of mine where I could jot down my feelings and dismiss all the loud noises in the house.

That short space of mine was a website online where I could vent about stuff, write about a potential future of an excellent old kind-hearted student, and all those things. I had gotten a couple of places to share my work for some 'awards' too.

Not to boast or anything, but someone here won a small award book kind of thing going on. I got second place, maybe not first, and that's completely fine. I was blissful when I saw the notification that they mentioned me in the results; I knew I had gotten someplace. And what do you do? Presented in front of me are my book cover and title!

I'm glad Abby Lee Miller wasn't there to clamour at me, yelling one of her iconic lines, "Second is the first to lose!".

But sometimes in life, these little things suddenly matter. I didn't care whether I won first, second, or third. Entering my book in a contest seemed like the biggest challenge. I was just too anxious about whether my book was qualified for something like this. It scared me to apply for awards that could end me up in court for not paying someone or something.

But one night, I gathered all of my courage and applied for it. Not even half an hour, I got a notification that it had accepted my book. That's when I felt how easy it is to pitch your books for unique content like this!

There seemed too many competitions, yet none of them seemed fitting for my book. Only a couple of them had the genre of my book. The idea of editing hit me. I asked other editors to edit my text, which panned out, making me lose multiple of the competitions.

I had probably asked inexperienced ones, so when I look for them now, I am extra careful to not fall for them again.

I had to put 'Under Editing' that demonstrated that I was rewriting my book. Until now, I haven't changed a word. There have been lots of events. And each of them took time away from me, trying to wrap it up.

That's when I understood something that had changed my full perspective on everything. Whether I am good at my pastimes, it loosens me up. It brings me a smile. I think after writing, I understood the accurate definition of a hobby. It's an activity you enjoy, not an act you perfect.

It was something I turned to when I was unsure of my feelings. When I was feeling anxious about action, I was about to do. It relieved me when I needed assurance. It made me rethink all my wrongdoings.

A book contained everything from your contact lists to tearfully writing a sad day. Maybe books are better than friends. At least, they don't spill your secrets to their friends.

I relish listening to music and writing a poem. The song 'The Moon Is Close Yet So Far Away', a cover by the artist K. is very comforting. That song has crept to my most played playlist. A very soothing voice and in the middle of the loving song, I could hear the guitar. I could listen to it day in and day out.

'Day In' is another song I fell in love with for a couple of months. I was glad to see the artist, Stephanie finally getting her recognition. I loved it to a million. I remember playing the song a hundred times while walking in my backyard.

The green plants in front of me with small white flowers decorating it seemed too perfect with this fantastic song playing in my earbuds.

Stephanie's voice is just so sweet. The advertisements where honey is being advertised and love are like dripping from the spoon? Her voice is like honey.

If you like writing while hearing music, consider me as your friend. I probably won't talk to you if you ever see each other, but I promise I don't sound as mean as I look.

Or maybe I am, and I just deny it. Everyone in Middle School told me how deliberate I looked. Anne was the first who shared her first impression, and I remember how taken aback I was. I was trying to smile and seem somewhat lovely to my classmates.

Anne was a good friend of mine. Though we both had our complications in the one year, we spent together, and she was an unforgettable friend. She enjoyed challenging herself and was quite confident of proving to our Math teacher that she is a distinguished student.

Speaking of Math, the last year of Middle School was terrible. I was striving terribly at it. Of course, my teacher helped me with every procedure she knew. She got me extra material worksheets, some useful websites, and a couple of diary notes for my parents to sign. Yet none of them worked out.

It was by my side. I used to come home, have my lunch, and sleep till six or seven. And watch my beloved shows from eight to eleven before trying to sleep. But nothing would work out. Those materials were just as brand new. Looking back, I missed some points. I could have improved my quick calculations by today and would have difficulty multiplying the table of seven.

And the next I used to come with some excuse not to answer the questions which they asked me to do. Sometimes it would work, and they would understand pardoning me from asking any more doubts. While sometimes they would tell me I do not convince them with my excuse, so I would have to confess to them and not talk the whole day.

I was the champion of procrastination. I loved history and a little Science, but Math was something I just couldn't wrap my head around. I didn't find the need for learning a + b the whole square.

I was so interested in learning Psychology online from a few different courses that I forgot to learn from the classes that would make me pass school. I had once passed Maths class only by half a mark. I was taken aback, looking at my paper with my mouth open. Masey, who was my 'study buddy' for Maths class, saw my expression and came close to me. She had seen my grade and put her arm around my shoulder.

"It's okay, Ashley. You will do better next time", she tried to comfort me. But I couldn't be settled by just words. I knew that no matter what, I will do better the next time. But what about now? What will I tell my parents today?

It was time to go home anyway. I swallowed and blinked away my tears. Masey probably noticed this and said, "Are you okay? Do you want to go and get a drink?". I shook my head and had seen my father was out there. The moment he asked me how was my grade, it was waterworks. I was sobbing in front of other parents and kids, with Masey out there.

My dad tried to calm me while we went to the car. "It's okay, don't cry." I blurted out how I was passed only by a mere half-point. He didn't say anything about my grade. Instead, he comforted me with his words. That night, he took me out to a mall. He knew I was weak in maths, and that's why he wanted me to take my mind off.

I was awake the whole night and was crying. I went downstairs to get a glass of water that would help me to go to sleep. I heard my mom and dad speaking.

"You know, I appreciate you taking our daughter out for clearing her mind but remember to make her learn that it's okay to make mistakes but at the same time, try harder the next time."

"I know, I know. Ashley had cried because of her grades. I couldn't let my daughter be sad because of just mere grades and numbers. She was stressed this time, she did everything in her power to higher those marks, but it didn't work out. She just needs some guidance in her studies, that's all."

I went upstairs and dropped my head on my pillow. I cried again this time, but not for the failing marks of Math but rather for the love and gratitude of my parents.

Middle School was a mess.

Chapter Five

I enjoy bluffing. There, I said it. I mean, come on. Have you ever seen a teenage girl in her days where she is up high soaring with passion but also days where she crumbles the moment she is yelled at because of a silly mistake?

I can't say I am susceptible only because I annoy everyone back if they do. Or maybe disagree with those who say these statements. But at the same time, if someone talks about my appearance, I just want to dig a hole and situate myself in. Tears pool into my eyes, while I try to look at the distant items for no one to notice my tears.

I think comparing two individuals might sound good to say, but the ones who are being talked to, those talks might just weaken them. Being frequently distinguished from any individual is exhausting. If it's studying, there is always that one girl who used to ace every exam. After they distribute the test papers, all the teachers say is how we should infer them as our role models and how we should strive to be like her.

If it's regarding personality, there is that one girl who knows how to do duties has a terrific personality, and is appreciative. I always thought I would never be enough for the world. Because no matter what I did, it seemed never enough to wow anyone.

I can be enthusiastic, and when I put my heart into something that I love and admire, I can achieve. Let's take my education as an example. That's something I have overlooked until seventh grade. When I say I was awful at studying, I mean it.

I couldn't go without a spelling error that lasted from fifth grade to sixth. I was horrible at math because of my sluggish personality. I wouldn't even complete my assignments until a class before the subject that gave me the project. I couldn't comprehend application-based questions, and it was the section I had lost a lot of marks throughout my school.

I think that's enough of downgrading myself, and I will lift the mood by saying, I tried. I tried changing a majority of these things, and when I say I saw profound changes. Giving yourself a pep talk is what I think pushes someone forward. If we can give our friends that same talk when they get lower marks, why are we unable to do it to ourselves?

As I mentioned at the beginning of the chapter, I like to bluff. Whenever there is this little encouraging change in me, I just have to show off to all I know. The energy just busts in me, and I roam around letting out high-pitched screams.

During the middle of my seventh grade, I gathered all my courage and went to my English teacher, one of the most amazing teachers I have ever seen. I walked towards the desk when she was sitting on the chair after correcting everyone's notebooks.

It was a notebook checking week. I had also gone to my teacher to spare some time as I had not completed my notebook work. I just had to play that one game last night. And that turned into multiple, which also ended up with me losing my time in writing my incomplete notes.

I asked in almost a whisper, "Excuse me, may I ask you something?". By the time, my cheeks were red as a beet, as it was my first time asking a teacher's help in front of like thirty other students. All eyes seemed to be on me as all others were sitting down with a paper in front of them; they had to return in about twenty minutes.

"Yes, is there anything you want to tell me?" she asked me in her soft voice, I had never felt more relaxed. I felt comfortable asking her all my doubts as I had many times before.

I continued, a little more confident now. I felt that spruce of enthusiasm now in me. I took my notebook from my side and placed it right under her eyes and asked my instructor to show me how I can improve my handwriting from simple letters to full-fledged cursive letters.

She smiled sweetly at me before picking my purple ink pen and showed me her ways of improving my handwriting. She grabbed it up, almost too elegant, and her hands worked on the paper.

"When you want to enhance your handwriting, start with the basics. Write your name, for example. 'My name is Ashley'. Keep on practicing this statement around five times then make another sentence, do this for a couple of months and you will see a drastic change. This is how we write the letter 'r', 'f'."

She helped me out with the most basic instructions ever. It was like teaching a baby to take baby steps to start walking gradually. She didn't promptly just give me tips and ask me to sit on my seat. But she took the little time she had and helped me out with writing.

And what do you know? I was practising my handwriting during one of the random notebook checking routines and my notes were complete, so I didn't have to run around asking for letters. She came and looked at my book; I got flustered and covered my book while smiling shyly at her, saying that I am timid and that I hadn't done an excellent job.

She removed my hand and took a view of my book. While, on the other hand, my cheeks were flushing red, and covered my face with my sweater paws and tapped on to it gently to stop the blood flushing towards it. My theory of the blood flowing didn't work, but it didn't cover a portion of my cheeks.

She stood there looking at it before patting me on the back, saying that I had done an excellent job. I bow my head down and look at the floor before thanking her. I felt that piece of my confidence return to me in that class. I cut one more task out of my checklist.

Year's later, I am still thankful to her. I was struggling terribly with my handwriting and it almost felt like I was a toddler who stumbled upon Middle School. She helped me regain my confidence in my handwriting.

Now, if you didn't already know, I wasn't a perfect student. So, how did I master my handwriting?

It takes a minor change in yourself.

Chapter Six

How did I make my handwriting turn from an elementary student to a high schooler?

First, it would be to sit with yourself and know your shortcomings. You can work on your fears rather than overlooking them. Knowing your drawbacks and turning them into your stability makes someone stronger.

Intimidation is what one feels when they have to do a particular action. Therefore, many lags, as they are not too aware of the outcome. They can't foresee whether it would be favourable.

You can't just recognize it and lay down on your bed feeling hopeful. You need to work on it instantly. 'If there is a will, there is a way', a quote my Science teacher has said throughout my freshman year in high school. I'm glad she shared this quote, and I have learned to use this effectively.

I practised whenever my chores bored me or had nothing to do. I thought of all the little times when I had finished my chores after whining for quite a while. Or laying on my bed, tired from staring at the white ceiling instead of completing my assignments.

We can remove these excessive times and fill it with all the pastimes you can do. However, it is okay to feel weary occasionally. You don't have to urge yourself to work more than you can.

There is no need for a healthy body if you don't have a healthy mind.

This is different for every individual. Some have quicker and those who take a longer time. You can compare yourself to others, only if you want to hurt yourself.

When you try something, you need a little enthusiasm. So what would I do? I would make myself excited and try to persuade my dad that we both need to go out there and buy an ink pen to practice my handwriting.

A purple colour pen with a straightforward glass design was my gift for that semester. My dad brought me multiple of the coloured pens, and yet the way I had used them was utterly disreputable. One pen dad bought me, and the cap was a little loose. And so I thought, why not take the weapon that produces hot sticky saliva and apply it to the pen cap?

If you didn't understand the clue, it was a hot glue gun. I applied all over the pen and stuck it to the barrel of the ink pen. And once it cooled down, I tried to open it only for it to stick to the cartridge forever. Hot glue can usually be relatively easy to remove, but I don't know what the case with this one was. I think I glued the cartridge of the pen to the cap. Or maybe I squeezed some all over the perimeter of the lid.

I remember having the guts even to ask my dad such a witless question about why it wouldn't open. Whenever I think about this day, I would scratch the back of my head and touch my face in embarrassment.

"Dad, so I glued the cap to the barrel and now the cap wouldn't open", I asked slightly pouting. He motioned me to come closer and give him the pen.

A roar of laughter passed his lips before referring to the glued pen.

"It won't open because you glued it, silly!" he cracked into a fit of a laugh while I was being dejected about how I squandered a two bucks pen.

My dad patted me on the back and said, "I have seen no one do something as mindless as this! Don't worry, I will get you a new one but never repeat what you did today,". He said before going downstairs to have his dinner.

I remember just standing there almost numbly, and my mouth opens in shock. I demolished a new pen in a matter of minutes because of my silly mistake.

I went downstairs, had dinner, and went to bed. Wiped my fake tears and took a deep breath. I blinked away my tears when mom and dad came to check on me if I had slept or not.

We have this portrayal of being a crybaby stored deep into our minds. Whether we are crying for losing money, losing a loved one or for overflowing emotions, we are weak.

No one should cry. The term crying. We are told it is only to be used if we relate it to a newborn. Isn't it appealing to be a twenty-three-year-old woman and still weeping like a child?

Engraved are these statements by society? We need to change these. No wonder why the stats are frequently high on mental health issues. They teach us to bottle our sentiments and zip our lips.

It's quite liberating to see that the teachers were right. They told us we are the future of tomorrow. And gladly, we can see that. There is some more awareness esteeming this than ever. Posts are being shared about vulnerability.

Everyone now got the right idea of being a friend. A friend isn't the only one who you copy your homework from and never talk with them again. The role of a friend is also to check on them. You don't have to ask them directly whether they are feeling well. We ask specific questions indirectly.

You can begin a chat with them and talk about the start of your day. Although this issue has gained widespread attention, don't speak with the 'quiet' students only because you had felt wrong about them. We behave those students like pets at school.

I despise those who ask me a question and start talking about themselves. A good listener is a person who is appreciating. If one talks about how they had a terrible day, you shouldn't immediately be talking about how your day was worse or the best day ever. You have the role of giving them an ear to listen to and a shoulder to cry on.

Our class until the seventh was very delightful. Whenever a student used to cry, some used to bring a tissue for her to wipe her tears. Two or three used to console her while the rest of the class tried to cheer her up. I felt comfortable sharing my problems with them, and they all acted like my older sister thought I had made some mistakes I regret.

I looked forward to going to school for the past couple of months. I do like my new class, but then with those girls, I kind of grew up with them.

The new class, the teacher, was unique. She was one teacher that you could see that she truly loved her career and was passionate about it. It just felt different. Though they were funny and cheerful, it wasn't the same.

Some girls are just straight up the most pleasant humans you will ever meet. Ellina, I didn't disseminate with her too well. However, in high school, I texted and talked with her more.

And I have never regretted not talking with someone as much as I do with Ellina. She's witty, smart, and kind. She seems to have the characteristics of every girl character in every book and movie.

There are multiple times she has helped me with either my writing or my homework and I can never thank her enough for this. She is also very talented, from art to public speaking. It feels like she is the main character and we all are just living in her life.

Though we don't know each other in-depth, I hope I can remain friends with her for a long, long time.

Chapter Seven

Today, while looking at the things I owned I came across this little diary of mine. A small one, pink and baby blue as it's the background. The border consisted of sewing drawings. A tiny little compartment with a lock for the key to go in and unlock it.

Two owls of green and pink colour stood in the middle on top of the branch, while some glitter was sprinkled all over it. The back cover had a similar design except for the glitter. After years of writing in it, the ends have been spilt and has some fleck over it,

The pages have a colourful flower on one corner of the page with spaced lines. There are four sets of these pages. On the first page was a blank page.
I had stuck the flag of Odorn with bright stickers around the flag. Just below I had mentioned that nobody was allowed to touch it except Ashley and her family.

Underneath the passcode of who could touch it was my signature which I had used different coloured pens for every letter of my name. And then came all the diary entries. Since we were taught diary entries only at the end of Middle School, I then had my format of writing diary entries.

I would write which class I was on and shortly went on to describe my day, Reading some of the pages now, it mostly consisted of my times as an elementary student.

From how I scorned a friend of mine touching my hair to a few of the class notes I had written. We were learning about mammals and reptiles. I sometimes look back and wonder how could I actually get these topics difficult?

After elementary, middle school came. These were the pages where I had written about my friendships.

About either a friendly student who had just joined our class or how I felt about my friends passing over me while making new friendships. How I had given hope for any human friendship and declared that this diary was my only friend because a diary is always there.

I had made a list of the gifts I would give my cousins during their birthday or about trips to Odorn that had never happened. One of my pages about Odorn was very touching to me.

Hi, Diary.

Once again there are talks about going to Odorn. I know, I know. I should just give up at this point. I have to give up. But I just can't. Whenever my mom speaks to any of her sisters on the phone and I suddenly pop out of nowhere.

She would ask me, "When are you coming to Odorn?" I would tell them this summer. Both, my mom and my aunt chuckle and mom would tell me to go finish my homework.

I realized now that they were laughing because it will probably never happen. But we still have to have some faith, right? I already told dad that we had to get Ravin cosmetics.

She was recently getting into makeup. Ravin sent some pictures of her makeup, it was absolutely amazing.

Dad nodded his head and I came here to make a list!

Okay so for Ravin, we will need a makeup bag and some of those expensive lotions you see on tv. I am not sure how to convince dad into purchasing these so I might have to make another list for that.

I don't like Barry, he was always just teasing me and if I had to get him something, it would be rotten eggs.

And I also heard that Lydia was getting into dresses. Lydia is Barry's older sister. I wonder why Barry can't learn something from Lydia because she was an angel and Barry was a demon.

Lydia made this gorgeous dress for a wedding. It was a blue dress with the sleeves all puffed with lace and it was all handmade with a sewing machine and some cloth. Let me remind you, she is only fifteen.

So I will probably get her some more cloth for her to make dresses for herself.

Alright, Mom is making some cakes and I promised to help her get done. I'll speak to you soon.

Other than the young me not knowing how to write a diary entry and disliking Barry, it makes me sad. About the fact that I was so sure that I would be visiting Odorn once again. It's been sixteen years and I still haven't visited it.

There was this person on a news channel speaking and her words struck me that night. "Those who are inside Odorn are continuously trying to get out while those outside are praying day and night to see all those who are still inside".

Maybe. Maybe, there will be a day where I would be able to give Lydia her clothes, Ravin the makeup she liked and Barry, the rotten eggs.

I also think that everyone I know does not follow the rules of a diary entry. If someone is angry, sad or happy, no one takes the time to write the day, date and time.

Everyone would just spill their feelings in their diary similar to what one does while speaking. I prefer to write my impressions in a diary and speak about true events.

I learnt this during my school years that not everyone agrees with my thoughts and I don't want to state them again and again. It's like getting a good grade and showing it to everyone's face that, "Look, I got this". At some point, it becomes tiring.

I learnt that it was easier for me to talk about my feelings in-depth while writing. I found that writing makes me say what I want to a person much easier.

While speaking to someone regarding my feelings, I don't. I don't know how to convey my feelings. So I opt to not say anything at all.

But in writing, all words seem to get out easily. I can talk about my day in a park or how the maths exam was hard in the perfect sense.

Another reason why I never let out my feelings to anyone is also that I saw how my relatives talk. They would be talking about our school and when they would start. All these talks erupt while washing the dishes.

"I heard that school starts next week", one of them starts talking about. What I noticed throughout the years is that the person that usually starts the conversation is the one who starts all the mini quarrels.

"No, it starts two weeks later", one of them would interrupt. "That's what my husband told me". She gets all of the information regarding school events through her husband.

Another one joins and says, "No, isn't it tomorrow?". While

I would be in the middle. The only one who actually goes to school and knows that school won't start for another two months.

But they don't ask me. The conversation would just follow again and again while I immediately excuse myself the moment I finish my work.

It's awkward to see them arguing about their children's education while in reality, none of them really do know when it's going to start.

All I hope is that whenever I wash the dishes again, I don't hear these talks.

Chapter Eight

Once, I was asked to tell whether I was intelligent or smart. I was quiet for a while to think about this question. Both of the words had the same meaning, so I did not understand why my uncle Harold would ask. I just smiled and said, "I am both of them".

Then, I had thought I had given a very quirky answer, and I was proud of my answer as well. What I didn't know is that the entire family would get to know if my answer in a few hours. Uncle Harold had shared it with everyone in the dining room, and everyone left out vast roars of laughter. While I had put my head down, observed my food and my cheeks burning red.

I hadn't given a wrong and answer yet my family was amazed. There was a sudden boost of confidence in my answer that they had never seen before.

Growing up, I was a very loud kid and a very talkative one too.

We visited an old friend of my mother. Throughout dinner, the lady would look at me and give me looks to be quiet. I would babble all day about anything and everything.

After years that day, they had met once again in a park. Interestingly, they talked about the dinner that had happened years ago. She chuckled while looking at me, "You're daughter spoke a lot that day".

I looked at her, and she was widely grinning while I looked back to the cold orange drink in my hand. I had confirmed that she had disliked me and I had to stop speaking a lot. I did try, but there is so much going on around in a moment. There is a person who falls down the stairs, or I read something intriguing, all this information should be shared with my family.

The daughter of the old lady had become a member of our family a little later. For the grand occasion which was celebrated for the fact that we have a brand new member in our family, we decided to dedicate a dance for them.

I was a junior in middle school. I thought, 'Dancing is fun!'. That was the last time I had tried dancing. It was during the summer holidays, and we had planned to use these two months for dancing for the big event.

A lot of issues had occurred during summer vacations. I was told multiple times I would be cut off from their group because either the older kids were in an argument with Aaron. I wouldn't be able to get the dance moves as quickly as other students and didn't have a dance to memorize it as well.

Lizzie was the older cousin who had helped us with the dance while also continuously breaking down our confidence. She did like my other cousins since they could dance better and learn it faster. I would usually be the underdog and seeing it back now; it was apparent the only reason they took me in was that it was a family event.

After the night Lizzie and Aaron had a heated argument regarding their opinions, my other cousins told me. I was going to get kicked off because of Aaron. Supposedly, that night my aunt had asked me to give a type of pill to my uncle who had back problems.

I gulped and went downstairs, held the bottle tightly and opened the door. There was Lizzie, crying frantically. The moment she saw me, she started yelling, "You're not in the dance! Okay. so don't even try to come tomorrow". Her mother was calming her down while I simply left the medicine down and left the room.

Back then, I hated her so much for being angry at me for an argument that she had with my brother. The next day goes event worse as she called me down, to dance along with all my other cousins who were dancing partners than just to watch me and give their opinion.

I was the weakest in dance. When the music started, my eyes were roaming all around for someone to give at least just one clue of what I was doing. My cousins, who were younger than Lizzie, cheered me with their hopeful eyes, but I still forgot a few of the parts.

When the music ended, Lizzie sighed and turned off her phone. She came closer and wrapped her arms around others and said, "She still can't do a dance we learnt a month ago. How long will you take?". She turned around and asked me.

I looked down as I had no answer to give her. She sighed once again and went to sit in her seat. She quietly mumbled, "If we take her out, her mother will be behind my back". But, her twin Demy stood up and said, "No, she will learn it and will perform it excellently."

After that day, Demy had been my favourite. She was patient and thought mine faster than my 'classes' with Lizzie. I was young too back then; I was only ten years old. When that incident occurred, I had disliked the sixteen-year Lizzie so much.

My thoughts were all asking her one question as to why she would take out her anger in a girl who is much younger than her? I had never known what exactly was the reason behind Lizzie's and Aaron's fight. I felt she wanted to humiliate me in front of all my cousins in which she succeeded.

Looking back, I am grateful for the opportunity. I tried dancing, and well, it just wasn't my thing. There are lessons in life that you learn in a problematic way. I never wanted her to make fun of my dancing; however, she might have been distraught at my brother that she took it out on me. And it's okay because, at the end of this dancing journey and at the start of the wedding, she became her usual self around me.

She once was offended when we told her we shouldn't do a group dance since I felt we were becoming older and I didn't want to spend our holidays in an activity I didn't even enjoy. I had said this in the car ride yet, and it somehow reached Lizzie. That night, it was a special occasion, and we all had to dress up for this dinner. She walked past me to get a pair of scissors to ask me a question.

"I heard you didn't want to do another group dance. Is it because of me?" She asked as she looked through the drawer.

I wanted to yell 'yes', that she was the one who made hate dance, to never step in the dance circle. Yet all I did was smile and said, "Of course not. I just felt we were getting mature and didn't have to perform like that anymore". 'That' refers to the ways of making us dance.

She sat on the bed next to Demy, who was playing some game, and told her. "Did you hear her? She didn't want to do any dances because she is too 'mature'", she exclaimed to Demy who just sighed and looked at her, "Why can't you leave her alone? She is a child, and you're an adult now".

I gave out a little smile and Lizzie might have noticed it, who immediately asked me to leave the room, I left the room and closed it. For the next hour, they were arguing with each other. I was glad Demy had my back, but I felt bad for her too. They had argued because of my lack of dancing skills.

Lizzie always seemed to have held a grudge towards me even after leaving our home, which is no wonder as to why she blocked all ways of communication with me. I didn't expect her blocking me, but I didn't care. It's not like I would share her text every day saying, 'Good Morning Best Friend!'.

I dance now, but I have dropped dancing in a group. I dance alone in my room to get some of the calories removed, and I do it for fun. I dance around, and when I see the mirror, I move it out of my way.

It just reminds me of when I was practicing for that dance, I was forced to look at myself, and Lizzie looked at me while rubbing her face in anger. I am slowly getting used to two considerable mirrors in front of me, and I tried dancing. It was of great help! I was able to see what I am doing in a more generous view, and I got to know what steps I am doing wrong.

My shoulders are also very crunched when I dance, so I have to make sure I stand straight. I might have hated dancing back when I was younger, but now that interest is swimming back to me.

I started dancing again to lose some weight as I was gaining a lot of weight all of a sudden. I had started with Zumba and saw quite a lot of changes in a few months. And my interest in dancing was slowly coming back, and I started to do hip-hop.

Chapter Nine

A joint family. Who knew what troubles it would come with it. A joint family is fun, sometimes. All the late-night games and a round of roasting are delighted to think about. However, that happiness can last for a couple of hours only.

I have told my dad many times about how I want my room and have a little desk to put my books and gadgets on, sleep on my bed, and have a narrow nightstand beside it.

As a kid, I would show off all the time about how I would have several cars and the most significant rooms and house, how I go out often with my family every Sunday. I thought I had the perfect family and life.

What else of my needs do I not have? A school with thousands of students, an enormous mansion to live in, and an extensive amount of food. I had the best group of family living with me. Yet something didn't feel right.

But it's so easy to see something so magnificent change so quickly. When you are born into a society where everyone is expecting to be correct in each step you take and in a community where everyone should exceed anyone who comes before the competitor, the company threw me into the racetrack from a young age.

They want us to be a well-oiled machine. Ever since a young toddler, they want you to be the kid that started walking too quickly. As a teen, they want you to ace every exam and every quiz. As an adult, they want you to have a house, a stable job, and a car.

It didn't seem like they wanted you to have all these achievements. Instead, they needed you to have them. The relative's opinions were of more importance than your capabilities.

Being able to have good scores, completed assignments, have a sense of fashion, know how to do chores nicely and quickly, the etiquette of an elegant one and so much more. How do they not expect us to fall and take a breath?

Two loving parents brought me up; however, we weren't the only ones. Big houses came to a lot of chores. There were nights I would turn around to face the other side where no one would hear me or see me and imagine the consequences of the actions that were swimming in my head.

There were days I just wanted to lie down and scream at the top of my voice for everyone to hear what I wanted to say. There were days I wanted to be quiet. And they filled those days with questions of if I'm feeling well.

Failure was a word that no one wanted to accept.

I wanted to sleep. Curtains to be closed and the sun never rises again. To never move a finger again. It seemed familiar for me to expect these in life.

I realized at the age of twelve, and I didn't want big cars or expensive weekends—just a brief space for me to breathe. I was numb at times, but I had moved past that and plaster a small smile on my face to avoid any talks back home.

I had been so tired of the same constant question, "are you okay?". Only because I never knew the answer to those questions. Was I okay? Or is this another "phase" thing?

I tried to raise my concerns to those I thought would help me out and give me some advice. I decided that it was time for me to break out of my shell. And what did they do?

They blamed social media. They blame the dramas and shows for putting such thoughts in our minds while in reality; we base it on what we are facing in our daily lives.

The response they gave me seemed generic. It was what the schools had preached for years. It was all for the internet. Mind you, and I used to get my phone only for the weekend.

If I voice my opinion on something, the response is almost automatic like those robotic ones.

"We will look at it". Those five words are the only answer they give me when I'm feeling nothing. Those around me have tried their best to situate themselves out of this place; however, there is always something or someone holding us back.

Everyone was escaping. Individuals were jumping with joy, and a smile was always there. Yet when I looked at the mirror, all I could see was just another person trying to be here.

I want to complete my education and then be able to provide them with their wishes. I thought dreaming about my future would help me get out of this hole I had dug and put myself through.

And that night, I took out my diary and thought about all the places I wanted to go to. Or the more significant risks in life that I want to take.

I want to have a business of my own to produce goods I know I will have fun making and sell them in the market.

I enjoy stimulating items and wanting to create my line of something. Business sounds fun. Except for all the math-related questions, it's enjoyable. These seem straightforward, yet there is a lot of work that goes behind it.

I can't just make an item and wait for people themselves to come and buy whatever they like.

I always thought marketing was easy. I had gotten the definition of marketing wrong. Thinking marketing was just approaching customers to purchase your items.

I feel like the internet is a great help for these. Though I am no marketing professional myself, I have learned a thing or two online.

My dad, who owns a store, works eleven hours a day and gets calls from clients. One trait of my dad I admire is that he knows the line of work and personal life.

I have never seen my dad talk about his work during dinner. This is one of the many traits of my dad I want to have when I grow up. I don't want to talk about my work while eating my burger. It seems just to drag the mood down.

And lastly, I want to become a psychologist to raise more awareness about mental health issues. Why is it still being overlooked even today? It is sad to see so many young individuals' trust being broken because to whom they thought would help turned them down by blaming it on the emotions of a teenager.

What if, even if I move away, I would still be in that night? Will I always be afraid of what would happen next? Or will my confidence grow as slowly as the night passes the time to the sun? Where will I reach? The same dark place where I had no support? Make the same mistakes and not learn from them. Or am I going to grow from the mistakes and mature?

Learn from what I have done to craft a better statement about myself.

I can, and I will show that the new Ashley does not differ from the old Ashley. Everyone will be able to do what they want to.

During Science class, when they ask what the liquid that fills cells is? You fidget with your fingers, tuck a strand of hair back and play with the nib of the pen before taking a deep breath that is incorrect.

You wait for many days before the teacher gives your test back to see that you had gotten that question wrong. A deep sigh leaves your mouth, and you sit back and look at the paper one more time—the only red mark from the entire document that was the centre of the attention.

Putting your head down while stuffing your paper in your bag. You just had to make a mistake. There was not a day where you would not see full marks.

The next day, the same questions are being tested. A little more confident than yesterday, you write the right answer. A bell went out. "Cytoplasm!". Immediately noting it down on the paper and giving the paperback to the invigilator more happily.

In the next class, your teacher hands your paper to you, and a big smile occupies your face. 'No mistakes! That's a first!', you think while looking at the page one more time.

If you can learn in school, the advantages of making a mistake, then what are the odds that you won't somewhere else? Learning to be in a part of an organization starts at school, you know to deal with the ones around in school.

It is okay to make mistakes. In scenarios like this, not only do you learn the correct answer but that it is okay to make mistakes, which is more important than the answer to the Science Quiz.

Chapter Ten

One of the biggest mistakes I have made was not expressing myself clearly, and I still lack in that. As an individual, we need to say what goes in our mind and our heart to change our surroundings.

I just can't put my feelings in words. I used to stutter if I did. If it was during a time where I was teary-eyed, and someone was asking about my well-being, it would be waterworks.

Another mistake I had made was assuming things too quickly. I had lost a couple of friends because of this; when they were making something for me, I was overthinking about it. Evelyn and Lily were the only ones who could tolerate my foolish actions and still be noble friends today.

They have been with me through everything. I have known my friends since a young age, and though we argued for the smallest and dumbest things, they still could be with me. I laughed, cried, and ranted with them.

In my life, I have been told I am too energetic. I need to calm down. Or I am too quiet and almost dead like. Then I have been exposed to be happier around more. There doesn't seem to be a middle ground in how I act.

If I am happy, they think that I am overreacting and I need to stop laughing very often. At times, I don't know whether to be happy, sad or angry.

That's why I am myself. There are days I feel like I don't have to put out what I'm judging to everyone besides me or address them. Thankfully, I have an understanding family who allows me to go through these times and supports me when I feel this way.

They are usually quiet when I am on my mood swings. And right before sleeping, all you can hear is them imitating me and annoying me one last time before sleeping.

On the days where I'm energetic and want to have a great time, I clear my mind and make jokes and let loose of everything. In my mind, the way you feel is the way you look at particular objects and ponder away.

Some families don't work as my family does; they might take a longer time to accept who you are as an individual. Talk with them regarding the issue you are facing with them, not responding to your feelings.

Remember the famous quote "Keep calm", try to remember this quote while you are speaking your feelings with your friends, siblings, or partners. I had learned this tip from my sibling, Aaron.

He used to get upset at mom and dad for something they didn't think was healthy for him, and he was to huff and whine before slamming the door. Where did that take him? Grounded for a week. I wouldn't want to get grounded for a week.

I used to get grounded every week instead. My electronics were taken from the start of the week and were given back to me during the weekend. There are times they forget these rules about and they trust us. Before regretting their decisions, they take it back.

Doing chores. I despise them so much. I wonder if it would be better to have an older sister who would do them instead of me. I will do her errands, but I don't want to clean the house. This is the mindset I had when doing chores. It was just dull to clean up dirt in which I had no hand in doing!

Looking back and testing the way my sister does my errands, I think I'm better off being the elder sister. Being older also gives you a handful of advantages. When Kassie and I have a little bickering back and forth, I am asked most of the time to stop. Most of the time, since I'm the middle child, I'm told to be quiet because I'm younger or older.

Clothes. I once cried during thanksgiving because I didn't have any dress to wear. And so I exercised during the time from

Thanksgiving to Christmas. Lost a couple of pounds and two to three inches.

I remember looking at the mirror, smiling happily at the way my clothes fitted more loosely than before. It usually was the right fit, or it was a little tight on the sides. But that week, I could look in the mirror without hoping to be another person. I didn't stand in front of it and wished some of my features would just disappear because of how distracting it was whenever I tried new clothing.

It may not have been a tremendous success, but I felt good after completing the exercise. That is when I learned something important in my life; you don't need a shiny and expensive dress to feel good, your mindset of what you think about a particular thing changes you.

Because no matter what, it's not the dress that's not fitting, and it is our mindset that is dividing us from loving your bodies. If the dress is tight, get a better fitting dress. You don't have to change your entire body just for a piece of glossy cloth. Sucking in your stomach and sitting up straight to get rid of the tummy that comes when you put your back a little lower.

I wish I had learned this sooner. Maybe when I was eleven years old, when I gained a tremendous amount of weight in just a couple of months. Everyone told me to stop eating. To watch what I was eating. I would cry and cry with cookies stuffed in my mouth. I would swallow it and wipe my tears and promise myself to treat myself like a queen. Only to break down again the next day.

I had watched many creators; however, only a few had helped me embrace my body type as it is. Brooklynn with her quick clips of her dressing up in crop tops made me realize that it's okay for us to have fat around our belly.

Not everyone has a straight flat stomach, and that truly is okay. Brooklynn has a vast platform and millions of teenagers come there to watch her perform quick clips, and it is great to see so many of them get confident in their body type. Though some of their comments under her videos are heartbreaking to watch, millions of other words make up for it?

The whole concept of being thin, but not too light, has always been on the top of her head. You should be thin, but consider having some fat on your thighs. Healthy, but avoid having any fat on your thighs. No fat in your face. Big cheeks, what are you? A kid?

Thin! Your bones shouldn't be visible. Your rib cage shouldn't be looking if you are wearing crop tops. You need to be physically strong too. Petite is a word that is just not acceptable. Extra fat around your stomach is almost humiliating to see in the mirror.

Nothing is almost enough. No matter what, we satisfy no one with our bodies. That's why Brooklyn taught me that everybody is perfect in their way, and I love her for that.

Chapter Eleven

When there is a race in life, you don't have to follow the race just to reach where everyone else is. You can go at your own pace, be it slow or fast. I pride myself on being one of the most lifeless people to do simple mathematics calculations, yet also the fastest to do multitasking when I 'accidentally' forget about my chores.

Or when I forget to do my assignment and rush to the classroom and take out my textbook, trying to complete my notes (which most of the time I'm successful in). Teachers come in to take a peek, only to be entirely satisfied with my work. I pretend to be checking my notes when they come around when in truth, I am completing my notes for those five marks.

I don't see the need of getting first place in completing a question we give that. I understand that writing in time is a skill one should have. However, to put down others only to praise the winners is wrong in my eyes. So I dislike it the moment someone says, "Let's see who does it first".

From time calculated questions to the big rush of the cities, there is just no time. Everyone wants to keep adding more numbers to their cards, so much that they forget to take a breath in the middle and to care for themselves. Being number one does not bring every ounce of happiness.

There is another issue of mine that I want to speak on that has derived my family members crazy. I'm additionally one of the most conclusive individuals ever. If you ask me whether you look good in blue or red, you would have to want a fast-forward button. I take forever to make a choice, and when I do; I make some pretty excellent choices.

For instance, I purchased this truly charming light yellow shirt which costs somewhat more than my standard cost, and of course, that is the shirt I wear frequently.

If you ask me to decide between blue or red, all you can see is me scratching my head and smiling awkwardly, not knowing what to do. I will pat you on the back and ask you to find it yourself.

There are times when I hate shopping. Due to my bigger size, clothes for those age range does not even fit my arms. When that happens, I just stomp my feet in annoyance, losing all the energy to look for more clothes.

Everything would either be too big or too small. There was just no perfect fit, which makes me compare myself to the other girls who would come, choose a pair of jeans and it would fit them perfectly.

Don't get saddened by a colourful dress that does not have your size, go to another corner and you might find a gem or if you find nothing at all, go to another shop. My mood would always be down when I used to go shopping. There would be this white shirt with daisy mesh sleeves only for it to be the smallest size and a crop top.

Or when I see a lovely dress, and it probably wouldn't even fit my arms. I grew conscious of my body and wanted to quit shopping and just go home. I sometimes would curse myself for having such an unhealthy body where everyone was tight and skinny, and I had fat hanging out.

One thing I would love to do when I want to grow up is to have an online business. The thought of having my little shop virtually always excites me. I want to grow my label, and I want to push forward myself into an enormous challenge.

I want to do a nonprofit business once I have grown it enough. To be the CEO of my small brand. Packaging and labelling each of my orders. The thought of doing that excites me, but I know that comes with enormous risks.

As a teenager, I would watch growing lip gloss business videos all day. I had learned two tricks and tips through these videos. I always had thought promoting an item was embarrassing. Ask everyone to look at your products. I would probably feel my cheeks blushing red as cherries.

Throughout these videos, I realized how important promoting is for showcasing your items. Almost all videos include this point. Many big labels also do it with YouTube ads, street posters, or they put it high while driving you can notice two or three of them.

But there is something else, too. I also want to become a psychologist. To help those around me. I had read somewhere that there were a couple of individuals who didn't ask their clients to pay them any money; I want to adopt that thought in my career.

I want to open a branch in Odorn. Torn by war and fighting. I recently found out that there was no money spent on mental health and is being lighted. I want to reach my hand out and help them.

It bewildered me when I had found this piece of information. The country is being aided. The war must have had a toll on the citizen's mental health. Every day and every night, they must be tired of hearing deadly screamings. They pass it between the lips of the martyrs. It truly is saddening.

I want to be a small light for those who are being distressed. I want to be a young star in their dark night, and I want to raise the heads of those below and raise their chins a little more confident.

Everyone deserves to smile after having a dinner full of nutrients. For the dishes to have all taste from salty to sweet. To drink clean water without any impurities in it just to keep going.

We can't forever wait for them to stand on their legs. A little hand in help won't reduce us from anything. Those who do good will be rewarded in any other fields that help might not come in the form of cash but maybe in happiness. The happiness of seeing a young child having to eat soft bread after weeks of starvation.

Maybe the problems of this world never get over with. There will always be an issue from our minds to bodies to the community. If we work together with similar aims but unique solutions, we might see the bright light.

Chapter Twelve

Each teenager has their own key. A key that would open their feelings, contemplations, and sentiments. Some need to finish their schooling, to go to a legitimate school and procure their degrees. Few of us would remove ourselves from school to pursue our fantasies before we actually succeed. Eventually, we, as a whole, have our imaginations, a lot that is put away in our hearts.

Nearly all questions I get asked about my future are not about the goals I prefer to achieve, instead of the gifts I wish to receive. They ask me," what is Something that makes your heart go crazy. Something that makes you in awe?". They answer it for me, "the new Mercedes, or do you choose the usual journal with a pen packed with it?"

I mean, sure, give me a luxurious car. However, I grew up in a strict and disciplined family. I can see when someone is teasing me and when someone is really with me. So when they say interesting talks like these, I already know that they are just going with the flow.

I know what you are thinking. Who would choose a journal over a car? They offer me choices to just bother me up, a trick they have used for years on kids my age. I adore a pretty diary with a black pen over a ' Mercedes.' To provoke me up. Using an example of an expensive chic ride seems to be their answer.

This is an ancient joke in our family, and I just wish they would stop. Some younger kids always get the mark and give a quick response. The kids who are still getting so excited by these thoughts are probably new to the whole family system. You can't blame them. You told them you would get Something huge and what do you get them for their birthday, "Congratulations". Quit giving us bogus expectations since our adolescence.

If they were telling the truth, I think I may go in the car. No offence to all the books lying on my shelves right at the back having nothing to do. It's not that they are not crucial to me, I cherish them to the moon and back. The cold sweat drips down my neck. The trembling of my hand of the thought of destroying a diary by my exceptionally, very lower-than-average drawing skills. Whenever I try to hold a pencil in my hands, there will be tears drops visible on the paper.

On this page, I'll compose my fantasy once again to think back years after the fact to see the aspiring me. I will become Something that will ideally have the option to cover my tabs. Do a thing which I regard. I don't want to sit behind a desk. I scorn whether it pays me hundreds of thousands of dollars a year.

What is the fun in that if I waste my life? Work out Something which I know I dislike. I saw a video that changed my mind on this. They titled the video, "I will not sit behind a desk and make someone else rich." Well, too sad, I didn't watch the video.

It showcases the daydreams of my future in the previous chapters. The process I crave for completing my dreams. I design my goals in my mind; I wish to tick off. Important locations I need to go to. These little things of mine are the seldom pushes that keep me going, sweat harder, to receive what I had been daydreaming about.

Let's say I had a successful career. I'm able to do what I do. I achieved what I have written in my mind, and I painted a positive mindset. Those are all the aims I have in my life, my top three priorities on my bucket list.

Somewhere in Soulsand and, away from all the loud. I want to have a tiny house on a green plain full of fresh air. Beautiful colourful flowers on the side, giving it more colour. A little lake on the side of it, the reflections of the chill stony cliffs of them that could be seen without a doubt. The cold, snowy mountains blowing calm refreshing winds of air towards the home.

I want the experience of wearing soft cardigans and mom jeans with some boots. These dreams have been with me ever since I was a kid. I always wanted warm clothes to wear during winter, and I own very little because I don't live in a snowy place. However, if I was just given the opportunity, I would love to use it.

Settling down outside under the warm sun. The light rays can fall on our skin. The delicious smell of food coming from the kitchen while we stare at the clear blue sky with few clouds decorating it. And of course, daydreaming about anything that runs into my fantasy world.

The birds fly in the opposite direction to escape the cold winter and to reach a warmer home. Little giggles falling from Kassie and the soft rustling of the metal swings, with Aaron pushing her from behind.

She can't swing the swing by herself, and she usually needs someone to help her push from behind. The next activity I am about to tell you is Something only Aaron and I have in our family, swinging to the fullest potential. When we were younger, we were the highest ones in the house. The leaves would rustle, legs close to the tree.

There were days where I would fall. But all I would do was giggle and remove the sand from my knees. I would sit back on and start swinging again. As we grew up, there was less and less time for us to enjoy the beautiful park. It seemed too forced to go to the park for a picnic every Friday. Thankfully, that had stopped after twelve years of my life.

After a long relaxation and having our stomach filled with countless amounts of food and desserts, night time would roll around. Sitting on my bed watching the dark sky from my window with a notebook, a pen on my lap.

The deep sky that holds the brightest and smallest stars on its shoulders and picks them and makes it the highlight of the night that is what a supporting family should do. A kind friend that hugs and comforts you, the neighbour that bakes cookies to cheer you up, or just yourself.

There are some days I want to experience that seems quite unachievable. It very well may be a day I'm setting myself up for a contention or the day I completion school. There is likewise Something I long for a considerable amount. Meeting the ones that have and will consistently remain a cherished memory to me. I love folklore music and was one of the not many in fifth grade to think about it. Others in class didn't check it out.

I enjoy the message of their songs; they include a vast range of genres, and they all have a meaning behind it. Be it self love, respect, and women's empowerment, they seem to include everything. The way they include their fans in every activity they do, and they seem to support their fans just as much as their fans support them.

Another activity I wish to do is to enjoy waiting to sit on the wooden chairs with a wooden table in front of us to dive in. I could either be having some rice with a piece of chicken leg and some side salad. We only have beverages on Sunday nights as we consider it as the weekend. It's honestly so much more delightful. I genuinely love homemade pickles. They taste so much better and truthfully, they last longer. We usually have them made during summer, and it's like two enormous buckets of them.

I remember coming from school, and I would ask my aunts what they cook, and they would be like "rice". And I usually used to ask them to fill ours. It got to where I would enter the kitchen, and they would be, "I filled yours a ton!" jokingly.

I generally get myself a bundle of a long straw of chocolate to treat myself for the tough week I had. My cousins consistently giggle alongside me when I discuss treating myself always.

Also, genuinely, everybody needs to have a go at doing that. Lift your spirits and rest comfortable thinking about yourselves. Barely any adoration, spoiling themselves with nail treatments and spa days. Few appreciate creating a sound for their followings—some need to sit someplace and draw their heart out.

White cloudy sheets tangled around my feet while an oversized sweater is on me. Writing what is on my mind and making a little poetry of them. Smiling gracefully and closing it, placing it on my nightstand. There is nothing better than after a long day throwing your back. Stretching your legs and arms. Yawning loudly before smiling widely.

Closing my eyes and making a brief prayer, "thank you for letting me breathe once again." I'm going to be grateful for all the individuals present in my life and those who aren't. Those who wish me well, even if they haven't met me. (Or if they want to ill, all I can say is 'ouch') It's okay to take breaks, to cry, and to not speak. It is okay to feel vulnerable. There is no such word as a 'crybaby' or 'weakling'.

They engrave those words in our minds by the weaker. Because those who are strong know that feeling low. Growing up, I could not bear to hear that word. And I made sure of it. I felt those words broke me. That it was like someone snatching my pride off of me.

There are days where I just want to close my eyes, and for everything to get quiet. For everyone to accept who I am. That it is okay for me to have flaws and make mistakes. I don't want to be perfect anymore, the student who tries to be first. I want to be me, Ashley. That youthful baby who was known for making a wreck.

Neither I don't want a fancy car nor a big luxurious house, *the key to my heart* is a quiet little place away from all the noisy urban areas. Maybe then, all of my dreams might come true.

About the Author

⸙

Zahra Abdul Razaq is a student and writer. She is an Afghan, born in Dubai. She currently studies in GEMS Our Own English High School, Dubai.

9 798581 432594